- Planning
- Trying to
- Want a ranch like Reagans?
- Gettin' ready for a down-home barbecue?
- Takin' your honey to a square dance?

Cowboy–English English–Cowboy Dictionary

Tex S. Ryder

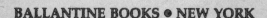

A Dana/Corwin Production

BALLANTINE BOOKS • NEW YORK

Library of Congress Catalog Card Number: 82-6660

ISBN 0-345-30155-2

Manufactured in the United States of America

First Edition: September 1982

Second Printing: October 1982

It happened. We all grew up to be cowboys. We have the hats, the boots, the hangovers, and all the other accessories. The only thing missing is the definitive work that clearly articulates the nuances and subtleties of the Cowboy language. With the publication of this book, we feel you will be convinced that that work is still missing. However, this tome is guaranteed to be as authentic as our hats, boots, and accessories . . . and a lot more fun than our hangovers.

Bill Dana

Contents

SIX erotic involvement

🥾 To some pokes **SIX** is an appetizer; to me it's a barbecue.

If I shrank from **SIX**, I'd be twelve inches tall.

I'm over-**SIX**ed and under-opportunitied.

RAISIN meaning

POPLAR having public acclaim

🥾 One **RAISIN SIX** is so **POPLAR** is that it's centrally located.

SIXY very provocative

🥾 She's so **SIXY** she could kiss the chrome off a Sears trailer hitch.

THANG quality

🥾 The best **THANG** about that critter is that when he's drunk he ain't sober.

DRANK a liquid refreshment

3

To some pokes SIX is an appetizer; to me
it's a barbecue.

LAUGH existence
(Bostonian pronunciation)

🐾My three favorite **THANGS** in **LAUGH** are a **DRANK** before and a cigarette after.

DAID deceased

BURRED interred

🐾Before I'd allow myself to be **BURRED** in a sheepherder's grave, I'd rather be **DAID**.

SHEE-UT Expression meaning, "Are you kidding?"

WAFFLE a willing spouse

🐾When I need breakfast, my **WAFFLE** make it.

SHEE-UT Expression meaning, "That's strange!"

HAH to have height

🐾Don't aim **HAH** if your ammo's low.

SHEE-UT Expression meaning, "I missed!"

BRAISE a gentle wind

🥾 That **BRAISE** was strong enough to blow the green off the grass.

SENSE in the period from a specified time in the past

🥾 **SENSE** I got hitched, I'm happier than a small bear in a big beehive.

TINSE uptight

🥾 There's a new tranquilizer. It don't relax you; it makes you enjoy being **TINSE**.

WAH an interrogation

🥾 Guide: We are now passing the Lone Star Brewery.
Cowboy: **WAH??**

PARCH   a covered forepart of a house; a veranda

🐾 If that lady was a house, I'd say her best feature was her **PARCH**.

STAPLE   a tall pointed tower on a church

🐾 That lawyer's got as many faces as a **STAPLE** has clocks.

SHEE-UT   Expression meaning, "Do tell!"

EIGHT   to consume for nourishment

🐾 I'm so hungry I could **EIGHT** a team of horses with their shoes on.

FLAY   a small parasitic insect

🐾 That **FLAY** was so rich he took a dog to work.

SHEE-UT   Expression meaning, "Ouch!"

8

Two can live as cheaply as one, if one
don't EIGHT.

LANE   to stand at an angle

🥾 Buster ain't a quick thinker. Why, he couldn't ad-lib a blister if he was to **LANE** against a red-hot stove.

SAME   the joining of two pieces of cloth

🥾 This quilt has more **SAMES** than Kansas has cows.

SHEE-UT   Expression meaning, "And that's the way it is."

SADDLE   a city in Washington state

🥾 I hear tell they got a mighty healthy climate in the Northwest. Why, in **SADDLE** they had to shoot a man just to start a cemetery.

WANED   having completed nursing

🥾 Don't trifle with me, now. I was **WANED** by a wolf and raised by a rattler with a toothache.

10

LAIG lower appendage, used for locomotion

🐾 He was so bow-**LAIG**ed, him and a knock-kneed lady spelled *ox.*

FANGERS digits

SANDPIPER an abrasive substance used for smoothing

🐾 He was such a terrible safe-cracker he had to **SANDPIPER** his **FANGERS** to open a conversation.

TROD attempted

🐾 He **TROD** to count to twelve, but he couldn't get his shoes off.

SHEE-UT Expression meaning, "That's dumb!"

LAHN filament carrying current

MAHLS measurement of distance

🐾 I'd lay forty **MAHLS** of communication **LAHN** under combat conditions to hear her burp on the phone.

SHEE-UT Expression meaning, "Tell it like it is!"

MAKE deficient in spirit or courage

🐾 The **MAKE** shall inherit the earth, but they won't get the oil rights.

SHEE-UT Expression meaning, "Who said so?"

11

He was such a terrible safe cracker he had to SANDPIPER his FANGERS to open a conversation.

SCRANE   to filter out

EWES   to have a purpose

🐾 He's about as much **EWES** as a **SCRANE** door on a submarine.

ODD   I would

🐾 **ODD** rather have a bottle in front of me than a frontal lobotomy.

DALSE   a large city in Texas, sometimes called Big D

🐾 In **DALSE** the girls are good-looking and the boys are looking good.

BURROCRAT   a government employee

🐾 A camel is a horse designed by a **BURRO-CRAT**.

PORE   lacking money

🐾 They were so **PORE**, they couldn't afford a watchdog. So they trained a cockroach to bark.

SHEE-UT   Expression meaning, "It takes all kinds to make a world."

MAMMA   maternal parent

🐾 **MAMMA**'s yearning capacity is greater than papa's earning capacity.

14

WHALE   a circular object held together by spokes

🥾 Ma loves the spinnin' **WHALE**. Just last night she won fifty dollars on the red.

FLAR   milled wheat

🥾 They were so **PORE**, they survived on sponge cake. They sponged the eggs, and they sponged the **FLAR**. . . .

SHEE-UT   Expression meaning, "That's delicious!"

BOB'LL SCHOOL   Sunday-morning instruction for children

🥾 I'm sorry I missed **BOB'LL SCHOOL**; my pa made me stay home and mark the playing cards.

STAID   a spirited horse; stallion

That corral was where my stud **STAID** stayed.

RARE   the back part

🥾 From the **RARE** she looks like two pigs fightin' to get out of a gunnysack.

SHEE-UT   Expression meaning, "How'd you like to have that comin' across the sheets at you."

PLY   a stage presentation

Ma loves the spinnin' WHALE. Just last
night she won fifty dollars on the red.

PLAYS the imperative used to express a polite request

🥾 Would you **PLAYS** remove your hat so I can see the **PLY**?

SHEE-UT Expression meaning, "Are you out of your mind?"

DRAP to let fall

ARMAGEDDON a declaration of independence

🥾 When they **DRAP** that bomb, **ARMAGEDDON** out of here.

SHEE-UT Expression meaning, "Whoops!"

PAR force

🥾 To me, white **PAR** is milk of magnesia.

SHEE-UT Expression meaning, "Smile when you say that, podner."

THOO to have cast

🥾 I joined the war on poverty; I **THOO** a hand grenade at a beggar.

SHEE-UT Expression meaning, "I needed that."

SAN ANTONE a town that lost its final "io"

🥾 I left my heart in San Francisco and my liver in **SAN ANTONE**.

SHEE-UT Expression meaning, "That's disgusting!"

NOZER a polite negative response to a male

YEZER a polite positive response to a male

YESSM a polite positive response to a female

NOME a polite negative response to a female

ELFIN a huge-tusked mammal

BOOF a small structure

🐾 He's so stupid he couldn't find an **ELFIN** in a telephone **BOOF**.

FEUDAL of no use, to no purpose

🐾 As **FEUDAL** as haulin' wheat to Wichita.

SPORE   very inept

🥾 His aim **SPORE** he couldn't hit a bull in the butt with a bass fiddle.

TRACK   to entice

🥾 A good yarn should be like a bikini: colorful enough to **TRACK** attention and brief enough to be interesting.

GRACE   a viscous, oily lubricating substance

🥾 It's the squeeky wheel that gets the **GRACE**.

DE SADE   to make a choice

🥾 He couldn't **DE SADE** whether to **SHEE-UT** or go blind.

SHEE-UT   Expression meaning, "I pass."

He's so stupid he couldn't find an ELFIN
in a telephone BOOF.

FAILURE   to touch that which belongs to another

🥾 If I **FAILURE** body, will you hold it against me?

SHEE-UT   Expression meaning, "Go figure out women."

TARE   a drop of liquid secreted from the eye

🥾 He was the most sorrowful man I ever met; he could coax **TARES** from a banker.

BOARD   to have on loan for a specific period of time

🥾 I didn't exactly steal it; I just **BOARD** it for keeps.

HATED   overly warm

🥾 **HATED** arguments cool friendships.

TELL   with extreme force

BITE   something used to lure fish

BAIT   to strike repeatedly

🐾 My paw **BAIT TELL** out of me for usin' the wrong **BITE**.

SHEE-UT   Expression meaning, "I bet you do."

MAJOR   a task done in the past

🐾 Who **MAJOR** outfit?

MAIN   cruel or abusive

🐾 My wife is so **MAIN**, when she **BAITS** me around the house, she **BAITS** me around the house.

ORGAN   the state bordering Washington

🐾 My sister lives in Ternal, **ORGAN**.

RAFFLE   a weapon

🐾 This is my **RAFFLE**, this is my gun. This is for fighting, this is for fun.

SAGE   a military blockade.

🐾 The **SAGE** of the Alamo was in 1836, remember?

HARES   observes audibly

🐾 She's so pure, she blushes when she **HARES** the word *intersection*.

She's so pure, she blushes when she
HARES the word intersection.

SHEE-UT Expression meaning, "I'm in love."

TARRED exhausted

🥾 I'm so **TARRED**, I could sleep for a week.

WARD a thing spoken

🥾 My **WARD** is my bond.

WAR to don

🥾 She's so fat she's got to **WAR** a girdle to get into her moo-moo.

She's so fat she's got a WAR a girdle to get into her moo-moo.

WAKE lacking strength

🥾 He's as **WAKE** as a kitten with rickets.

TOAD having communicated orally

🥾 If I **TOAD** you once, I've **TOAD** you a hundred times—don't clean frogs in the house!

SHEE-UT Expression meaning, "That's too sour."

PALE to remove an outer covering

🥾 His breath could **PALE** the skin off an onion at thirty paces.

If I TOAD you once, I've TOAD you a
hundred times—don't clean frogs in the
house!

NAILING resting on the knees

🍪 We caught her **NAILING** in front of the preacher, but she wasn't exactly petitioning the lord.

JITS thrust-powered aircrafts

FASS speedy

🍪 Them new **JITS** is so **FASS**, one of 'em took off for New York with two rabbits and landed with two rabbits.

ATE to consume

SAHDWISE with the long part parallel

🍪 Her mouth's so big, she can **ATE** a banana **SAHDWISE**.

PURTY very attractive

TIMPACHOOR body-heat measurement

🍪 That nurse was so **PURTY**, when she took a **TIMPACHOOR** she had to discount 25 percent for proximity.

WARRS is concerned with

MANK a fur-bearing rodent

🍪 That rich old lady **WARRS** so much, she has **MANK** ulcers.

We caught her NAILING in front of the preacher, and she wasn't exactly petitioning the lord.

MATE the flesh of animals, used as food

🐾 One man's **MATE** is another man's bison.

BARE an intoxicating liquid made from hops and barley

🐾 I don't drink **BARE**, I rent it.

SHARD a method of washing

🐾 I just **SHARD** last week; now I'm dirty again.

MERE a reflecting surface

🐾 She was so ugly that if she wanted to look in a **MERE**, she'd have to sneak up on it.

STARE an ox

🐾 He's as nervous as a **STARE** in a steakhouse.

NARRER limited in scope

🐾 Gals that walk the straight and **NARRER** are usually built that way.

WAHF female spouse

NAHT after dark

🐾 I was sure upset about Frank gettin' caught with Billy Bob's **WAHF** last **NAHT**. **NAHT** before, it could have been me!

LIGHT tardy

🥾 My girl friend said she was **LIGHT**. I said, "Do you mean tardy, or am I leavin' town?"

YUNGUNS children

TAYCHERS instructors

MAHLS measurement of distance

BORRY get the loan of

LIE-BERRY building that houses many books

🥾 When we was **YUNGUNS** the **TAYCHERS** told us Honest Abe would walk **MAHLS** to **BORRY** a book. Now they close the **LIE-BERRIES** on his birthday.

MYZIN astounding

🥾 To me the most **MYZIN THANG** is that wrong numbers are never busy.

TAHT very close to the skin

INSAHD the side closest to the skin

🥾 Her jeans is so **TAHT**, they wear out on the **INSAHD**.

37

One man's MATE is another man's bison.

FAHND to discover

HAPNIS joy

> 🐾 They say that lots of money won't bring **HAPNIS**, but I'd like to **FAHND** out for myself.

ESSERSAHZ vigorous body movements to promote health

> 🐾 I don't get much **ESSERSAHZ**. I get winded turnin' on the television.

English—
Cowboy

to sense **FAIL**

🐾 The higher a drunk **FAILS** in the evenin', the lower he **FAILS** in the mornin'.

to make a mistake **AIR**

🐾 To **AIR** is human, but it **FAILS** divine.

"Oh, am I happy!"
    SHEE-UT!

employed **HARD**

I had a beautiful HARD girl. Couldn't keep my hands off her. So I FARD the hands.

unemployed **FARD**

> 🕴️ I had a beautiful **HARD** girl. Couldn't keep my hands off her. So I **FARD** the hands.

"What'd you do that for?"   **SHEE-UT!**

a number between nine and eleven   **TIN**

an inhabitant of the Lone Star State   **TIXIN**

> 🕴️ A **TIXIN** will: I leave my son **TIN** million dollars, and he's lucky I didn't cut him out entirely.
>
> This here **TIXIN** bought two Rolls Royces and took his change in Cadillacs.

"How about that!"   **SHEE-UT!**

sincere expression   **TROOF**

> 🕴️ I have the greatest respect for the **TROOF**, so I only use it in emergencies.

a variety of green vegetable that grows in pods   **PAYS**

> 🕴️ I **EIGHT** my **PAYS** with honey,
> I've done so all my life;
> It makes the **PAYS** taste funny,
> But it **CAPES** 'em on my knife.

"Big deal!"   **SHEE-UT!**

optic organ **AH**

  🥾 The bull's **AH** is the last part of the target to
    wear out.

"T'warn't nothin' "
  SHEE-UT

strong spirits **ALKY-HAUL**

  🥾 That drunk needs more blood in his **ALKY-
    HAUL** stream.

alcoholic beverage **DRANK**

  🥾 **DRANK** should never be given to a man
    who's given to **DRANK**.

to consume food **EIGHT**

  🥾 Two can live as cheaply as one, if one don't
    EIGHT.

profound **DAPE**

  🥾 Beauty is skin **DAPE**, but ugly is to the bone.

obviate **A VODE**

> 🥾 **A VODE** a ruckus if possible, and specially **A VODE** 'em if impossible.

acquires **GITS**

> 🥾 Sometimes all the early bird **GITS** is up.

casts **THOSE**

> 🥾 When he's depressed, he **THOSE** hisself on the mercy of the quart.

a long distance **FUR**

> 🥾 A tenderfoot's got to be twice as good to go half as **FUR**.

24-hour period **DIE**

> 🥾 A **DIE** away from him's like a month in the country.

a large piece of land used for raising cattle **WRENCH**

> 🥾 They call him a tenderfoot at the dude **WRENCH**, but it ain't that end that's tender.

Expression meaning, "So what?" **SHEE-UT!**

Expression meaning, "That's hard to believe!" **SHEE-UT!**

brain **MINE**

He's so cheap he stays home and lets his **MINE** wander.

They call him a tenderfoot at the Dude WRENCH, but it ain't that end that's tender.

state in the Southwest **AIR ZONA**

🐾 In **AIR ZONA**, there are lots of towns that are so small the "welcome to" and "you are leaving" signs are back to back.

genuine **RAIL**

female offspring **DOUGHTER**

🐾 She was only a **RAIL** estate agent's **DOUGHTER**, but she gave a lot away.

lacking money **PORE**

🐾 We were so **PORE** when the wolf came to our door, he packed a lunch.

communicated orally **TOAD**

🐾 She has quite a past—and I'm **TOAD** it financed her present and future.

retains **CAPES**

🐾 He never loses his temper; he always **CAPES** it handy.

more than one seat **CHEERS**

🐾 I'm as nervous as a long-tailed cat in a room full of rockin' **CHEERS**.

to produce by elaborately combining various elements; to contrive **WAVE**

He could **WAVE** a dollar's worth of story out of a penny's worth of facts.

the Deity **LARD**

Here's bread, here's meat; for **LARD**'s sake, let's eat.

a man's name, derived from the Greek *petros*, meaning *rock* **PATER**

And when I get to heaven,
to Saint **PATER** I will tell,
"Another cow poke signin' in,
I've served my time in hell."

a continuance, or opportunity for continuance **LACE**

Here, take a swig of this joy juice, it'll give you a new **LACE** on life.

tired, exhausted **WARY**

I feel as **WARY** as a three-day horse on a five-day run.

Expression meaning
    "You better be kidding!"
      SHEE-UT!

"What am I supposed to do?"   SHEE-UT!

excessive warmth   HATE

  🥾 Talk about **HATE**; it's enough to melt a dog.

an occupation   BIDNIZ

  🥾 Her age is her **BIDNIZ**, and she's been in
    BIDNIZ a long time.

except on the condition that   LESSON

  🥾 There's nothing in the world better than the
    love of a good woman, **LESSON** it's the love
    of a bad woman.

"Do I love her?"   SHEE-UT!

to assign nomenclature to a female   **COLLAR**

🐾 They **COLLAR** Pepper, cause she's been through the mill.

a scornful expression   **SNARE**

🐾 That old maid loves to go to the theater. Don't **SNARE**, it's the only chance she'll get to walk down the aisle with a man.

implement used for sewing   **NATAL**

🐾 My brother's so skinny that when he closes one eye he looks like a **NATAL**.

jewelry worn on the finger   **RANG**

🐾 That gal is like a bathtub—she acquires one **RANG** after another.

"I'm rich."   **SHEE-UT!**

That gal is like a bathtub she acquires one
RANG after another.

well developed, sharp   CANE

🕭 Them gossips have a **CANE** sense of rumor.

cultured upbringing   **BRAIDING**

🕭 Her parents gave her **BRAIDING**, but she picked her own teeth.

irritating habit   **PAVE**

🕭 An Aggie's pet **PAVE** is using an ashtray before the floor is full.

to have viewed   **SANE**

🕭 I **SANE** better conversations in alphabet soup.

Her parents gave her BRAIDING, but she picked her own teeth.

repast **MAIL**

🥾 If it weren't for toothpicks, he wouldn't know what to do after a **MAIL**.

"That's too sweet." **SHEE-UT!**

to consist of specific words and phrases **RAIDS**

🥾 His tombstone **RAIDS**: Here lies Les Moore, four shots from a .44, no less, no more.

to sense visually; also, to comprehend **SAY**

🥾 I can't **SAY** wearin' gloves. It's cheaper to grow skin than to buy it.

"I coulda had a V-8"
   SHEE-UT!

If it weren't for toothpicks, he wouldn't
know what to do after a MAIL.

low slang for the nose   **BAKE**

> If I had a **BAKE** like yours, I could hang from a tree and wave with both hands.

a form of transport of goods   **FRIGHT**

> His face could make a **FRIGHT** train take a dirt road.

to touch   **FAIL**

> She was just a policeman's **DOUGHTER**, but you couldn't cop a **FAIL**.

straw   **HIGH**

> She was just a farmer's **DOUGHTER**, but she knew how to roll in the **HIGH**.

She was just a farmer's DOUGHTER, but
she knew how to roll in the HIGH.

attractiveness **A PAIL**

🐾 She was just a fruit vendor's **DOUGHTER**, but she certainly had **A PAIL**.

very unattractive **OGLY**

🐾 She's as **OGLY** as **TIN** miles of bad road.

"Smile when you say that, pard." **SHEE-UT!**

a season of the year **SPRANG**

🐾 They weren't very clean; why they'd start **SPRANG** cleanin' by throwin' out the Christmas tree.

a floral tribute **RAITH**

🐾 One winter a mouse got electrocuted in the barn. Every year we put a **RAITH** on the fuse box.

a youngin' **ENFUN**

🐾 When I asked her how she could have a child that age, she said she didn't; when she had him, he was just an **ENFUN**.

"How'd you guess?" **SHEE-UT!**

leafy vegetables **GRAINS**

🐾 Next door to my uncle's was a widow tendin' her own farm. They grew peas, **GRAINS** and friendly.

She was just a fruit vendor's DAUGHTER,
but she certainly had A PAIL.

largest city in Louisiana **NORLENS**

> 🦪 My cousin's with the FBI now—they caught him in **NORLENS**.

to take temporarily **BARS**

> 🦪 If he smokes your cigars, lets you pay the check, and flirts with your wife, he's your pal. If he also **BARS** your car and sleeps in your bed . . . then he's a relative.

possessive pronoun, second person singular or plural **YORE**

> 🦪 Don't put on **YORE** swimsuit, darlin'; it ain't that kind of dive.

number between five and seven **SEX**

> 🦪 Why he'd never steal; he worked in a bathhouse for **SEX** years and never took a bath.

unethical practice **CHATIN'**

> 🦪 The most common causes of **CHATIN'** are slow horses and fast women.

"Saved by the bell."
SHEE-UT!

one who doesn't tell the truth   **LAR**

I caught a catfish so big I got up in the middle of the night and called myself a **LAR**.

to effuse blood   **BLADE**

He's so sensitive, he'd **BLADE** if you used a sharp tone of voice.

financially embarrassed   **BUSTID**

If Dolly Parton was a farmer, she'd be flat **BUSTID**.

If Dolly Parton was a farmer; she's be flat
BUSTID

"Now that's my
style."   **SHEE-UT!**

being at rest   **ASETTIN**

It was so cold I was **ASETTIN** like a monkey
ballin' a football.

behave towards   **TRAIT**

Catch 'em young, **TRAIT** 'em rough, tell 'em
nothin'.

to take the property of another; to rob   **STALE**

He'd **STALE** the oink from the pig.

an area of study; also a pasture   **FAILED**

Here's to Farmer Jones, a man outstanding in
his **FAILED**.

"That's fascinating."   **SHEE-UT!**

the ratio of distance traveled over a given length of
time **SPADE**

👢 He ran with the **SPADE** of a scalded cat.

ill-humored, argumentative, misanthropic
MAIN

👢 As **MAIN** as a junkyard dog.

two or more draft animals harnessed together
TAME

👢 She's more stubborn than a **TAME** of mules
—and half as purty.

a liquor made from crushed grapes **WAN**

👢 Women are like **WAN**. Some are to be
sipped. Some are to be gulped. And some are
to be kept in the cellar.

"You and me bofe, podner." **SHEE-UT!**

dull, uninteresting **BORN**

👢 I never saw a more **BORN** person in all my
born days.

an old man **GAZER**

👢 That old **GAZER** can talk the berries off the
bush.

He ran with the SPADE of a scared cat.

without hair **BALL**

part of body between head and chest **KNICK**

🥾 He's so **BALL**, it looks like his **KNICK** is blowing bubble gum.

"Expression meaning,
    "Who couldn't?"
    SHEE-UT!

overindulgence in an activity **SPRAY**

🥾 I see Ma's been on a drinkin' **SPRAY**. I saw her lipstick on the still.

liquid made from hops and barley **BARE**

🥾 **BARE** doesn't drown your sorrows; it only irrigates them.

"You're full of it." **SHEE-UT!**

first-person plural pronoun **WAY**

🥾 **WAY** had a banker's cocktail. One drank, you lose interest; two dranks, you lose principle.

74

to gain office   **LECTID**

> 🥾 The trouble with political jokes is that some-
> times they get **LECTID**.

beyond her reach   **PASTOR**

> 🥾 She was only a minister's daughter, but I
> wouldn't put anything **PASTOR**.

a silhouette created by light   **SHADDER**

device for opening wine bottles   **COCKSKOO**

> 🥾 He's so crooked, he could stand in the
> **SHADDER** of a **COCKSKOO**.

"I swear, it's true."   **SHEE-UT!**

visual organs   **PAPERS**

> 🥾 JAPERS CRAPERS, where'd you get those
> **PAPERS?**

"That's weird."
   SHEE-UT!

a severe setback **LOSS TEVITHIN**

> 🥾 The tornado blew the farm away. We **LOSS TEVITHIN** but the mortgage.

law-enforcement officer **SHURF**

protection **KIVVER**

> 🥾 Our **SHURF** spends half his time runnin' for office and the other half runnin' for **KIVVER**.

male fowl **ROOSER**

> 🥾 AH crossed a **ROOSER** with another **ROOSER** and got a very cross **ROOSER**.

an individual or type **KARKTER**

flattering statement **COMPLIMEN**

cost of item **PRAHS**

> 🥾 That **KARKTER** called me a pig, but with the **PRAHS** of pork today, I took it as a **COMPLI-MEN**.

SHEE-UT also has the connotation:

- Are you kidding?
- Beats me.
- I can't believe it.
- Damn it.
- Damned if you do, damned if you don't.
- Wow!
- Aw, that's easy.
- You're kidding.
- You must be kidding.
- I give up.
- I never want to go through that again.
- How about that?
- Oh, no, you don't.
- Oh, am I happy!
- That's all she wrote.
- Watch out.
- Help!
- What the hell was that??
- That's strange.
- Watch out below.
- Who said so?
- Are you out of your mind?
- What a heartburn.
- That smarts.
- I need an Alka Seltzer.
- You hadda be there.

- Do I love her?
- We lost.
- We won.
- We broke even.
- I swear, it's true.
- It's about time.
- I pass.
- Back off, pardner.
- Where is everybody?
- That's too much.
- I'm gonna kick ass!
- Please, somebody up there, help me.
- Oh, *that's* what happened!
- Why didn't I think of that before?
- We are out of luck.
- I'm broke.
- I wish I could.
- Good riddance.
- Now, that's fast.
- I'm fed up.
- We blew it.
- That's delicious.
- I struck out.
- That's all she wrote.
- I'm beat.
- What happened?
- And that's the way it is.
- Did that really happen?
- Congratulations.
- I needed that.
- Man, it's hot.
- Boy, it's cold.
- What a beautiful day.
- Not so loud.
- What are you gonna do?
- That's horrible.
- That's clever.
- That's ridiculous.

- That's bewildering.
- That's too sour.
- That's too sweet.
- Do I have to get up this early?
- Oh, no. Not again.
- Saved by the bell.
- It costs that much?
- Hey, I can afford that.
- I'm rich.
- I lost it.
- I found it.
- Too late.
- Too early.
- That's relaxing.
- How'd you guess?
- No doubt about it.
- You're full of it.
- Well, if that's all you need.
- Why didn't I think of that?
- That's trashy.
- Let's have a drink.
- That's funny.
- That's tragic.
- That's dull.
- That's fascinating.
- What am I supposed to do?
- What can you do?
- Now, let me think that over.
- I'm confused.
- Nobody's gonna push me around.
- I've been swindled.

    . . . and horse manure.

TRIAL   a path leading off into the sunset

    Happy **TRIALS** to you . . .

Happy TRIALS to you . . .

Acknowledgments

Thanks to John Bates, Hennen Chambers, and Meg Staahl, members of the Light Stuff Company.

—Bill Dana, Editor